ORANGE FLOWER WATER

BY CRAIG WRIGHT

DRAMATISTS
PLAY SERVICE
INC.

ORANGE FLOWER WATER
Copyright © 2004, Craig Wright

All Rights Reserved

SPECIAL NOTE

For Beth Blickers

ORANGE FLOWER WATER was produced at the Contemporary American Theater Festival (Ed Herendeen, Founder and Producing Director; Catherine Irwin, Managing Director; David Wanger, Assistant Managing Director) in Shepherdstown, West Virginia, in July 2002. It was directed by Leah C. Gardiner; the set design was by Marius Henry; the lighting design was by Paul Whiteshaw; the sound design was by Kevin Lloyd; the costume design was by Daniel Urkle; the stage manager was Allison C. Wolooka; and the assistant stage manager was Danny Huernzal. The cast was as follows:

CATHY CALHOUN .... Mercedes Herrero
DAVID CALHOUN .... Jason Field
BETH YOUNGQUIST .... Libby West
BRAD YOUNGQUIST .... Paul Sparks

ORANGE FLOWER WATER was produced at The Jungle Theater in Minneapolis, Minnesota, in July 2002. It was directed by Bain Boehlke; the set design was by Bain Boehlke; the lighting design was by Barry Browning; the composer and sound designer was Victor Zupanc; the costume design was by Amelia Cheever; the production manager was Barry Browning; and the stage manager was Elizabeth R. MacNally. The cast was as follows:

CATHY CALHOUN .... Amy McDonald
DAVID CALHOUN .... Brian Goranson
BETH YOUNGQUIST .... Jennifer Blagen
BRAD YOUNGQUIST .... Terry Hempleman

CHARACTERS

DAVID, a pharmacist, 30s–40s

CATHY, a choir director, 30s–40s, wife of David

BRAD, owner of video rental stores, 30s–40s

BETH, wife of Brad, 30s–40s

SETTING

The time is the present. The play takes place in various locales in Pine City, a small town in north-central Minnesota. The set is a bed and bedside table and four chairs (at the edge of the playing space) on an otherwise bare stage. On the bedside table, there is a telephone and, throughout the entire play, a small stuffed orange tiger — ideally, a "Beanie Baby."

PERFORMANCE NOTE

The four chairs onstage are for the four actors and all the actors should be on stage and visible throughout the play. During the pre-set, at the top of the show, the stage should be dimly lit, with a gentle pool of light on the stuffed tiger. Once the show begins, no more special attention needs to be paid to it.

"It is the future generation that presses into being by means of these exuberant feelings and supersensible soap bubbles of ours."

—*Schopenhauer*

ORANGE FLOWER WATER

Scene 1

Music rises in the darkness. Light rises on Cathy.

CATHY. Dear David. Get ready. All three of the kids need to take lunches to school today. I have already made the sandwiches, but the rest needs to be assembled by yours truly. To make matters worse, Gus has early morning Math today as well, so you have to get him there by 7:30, come back and get the girls, and take them later. And try not to fight with Ruthie. If you wake her up early enough, it should all work out, and what I have found works with her is to let her choose the radio station in the car and then shut up. Annie has Brownies after school. As for dinner, you'll be pleased to know I have reached a new state of self-awareness and have not prepared anything, confident that you will be taking the children out for dinner tonight regardless of what the checkbook looks like. Have fun! Don't forget Gus has a soccer game on Saturday and Annie is going to Taylor's birthday party. Maybe you could take Ruthie to a movie? (Can you tell I'm concerned about you two?) Finally, and don't ask me why, the painters are coming on Sunday morning and the fumes are not good for the kids, so either go to church — ha ha — or take them out somewhere. I should be home by 5:00 P.M. Sunday afternoon. Please pick me up in the north parking lot of the school. The buses will all be in the south parking lot, but I need to go through the building to divest myself of all the accumulated crap these stupid choir festivals send you home with, so I'll come out the back door and wait for you there. Wish me luck! Cathy. P.S. I stood at the end of the bed this morning, once I was all dressed and ready to go, and the light was angling in from the hall, and you looked very sweet and innocent, very much the same young man who so charmingly and insinuatingly complimented my "nice music" so many years ago. I know we get very busy around here serving the three little Hitlers, but please know, if anything should happen to me this weekend, if for some strange reason, the bus drops through the bridge in Little Falls, or if I'm crushed to death by a mob of anxious sopranos, please know that I love you and feel ever so lucky and proud to be your wife in this strange and way-too-busy world we have procreated ourselves into. Yours more truly than truly can ever say … Cathy. *(Cathy exits the playing area and sits down.)*

Scene 2

David and Beth rise and enter the playing area. Beth lies on the bed and closes her eyes. David lies beside her and gently caresses her face.

DAVID. Now, I want you to put all thoughts of this world out of your mind.
BETH. David …
DAVID. *(Gently.)* Come on. "All thoughts of this world out of my mind."
BETH. *(After a beat.)* All thoughts of this world out of my mind.
DAVID. These four walls. The picturesque Holiday Haven Motel. The cars outside in the parking lot. Highway 59. It's all … pixelating, like little dots on a computer screen, it's all pixelating and slowly dissolving away … *(Beth opens her eyes to look at him.)* Shut your eyes.
BETH. But I think it's kinda cute the way you're … doing, you're … you're like a little gnome, making a spell.
DAVID. Thank you, that's my gnomish intent. Shut your eyes.
BETH. OK. *(He waves a hand over her eyes and she closes them; he kisses her eyelids and then continues with his spell.)*
DAVID. *(Quietly hypnotic.)* And now the whole town of Pine City — Lake Melissa, Sundberg's Café, The Sandwich Hut, The Voyageur — is all falling, falling through the clouds, dropping down through miles of clouds until you can't even see it anymore, Beth, it's a speck, and then it's not even a speck, it's gone. Goodbye,

Pine City.

BETH. *(After a beat.)* So where are we?

DAVID. We're in a bay in a kingdom in the clouds, and it's clear and it's quiet and it's beautiful ... and it's *just us.*

BETH. I like that.

DAVID. And in the distance ... *(He begins to unbutton her blouse very slowly. She opens her eyes.)*

BETH. *(Coy.)* What are you doing?

DAVID. In the distance —

BETH. *(Coy.)* I see what you're doing ...

DAVID. In the distance, we can see huge apples ...

BETH. Apples?

DAVID. Yes, apples ... *(He opens her bra, revealing her breasts.)* Apples as high as ... buildings, apples like two tall ships, floating on the water, golden and then shading into pink near the tops, and the sunlight and the mist, it's all like music, like the sweetest, quietest music, and we're there, and it's all ... it's all safe ... and quiet ... and cool.

BETH. I'm so sick of this hot summer.

DAVID. Me too. *(He kisses her breasts.)*

BETH. I finally got fed up the other day and bought a room air conditioner for the family room, it felt so extravagant, but —

DAVID. No, you deserve it —

BETH. They were on sale —

DAVID. Even if they weren't. Even if they weren't. *(Brief pause as he kisses her breasts. Then the conversation continues with intermittent kissing.)*

BETH. Tell me something.

DAVID. What?

BETH. Do you really love me as much as you *think* you do?

DAVID. I *think* so.

BETH. It doesn't seem possible.

DAVID. I don't think real love ever seems possible; it just is.

BETH. I'm serious, I worry sometimes ...

DAVID. Beth ... listen —

BETH. What?

DAVID. I don't know what's possible or impossible ...

BETH. I know.

DAVID. I'm *totally* out of touch with reality ...

BETH. I know.

DAVID. All I know is when I'm with you, I feel alive, I feel like the real history of my real life is really happening; and like I'm so lucky to be able to kiss you … and touch you … and be with you and be your partner, a little while … on the way … you know? *(He reaches behind her to unzip her skirt.)*

BETH. Wait a minute.

DAVID. What? What do you want? Wine? *(Insinuatingly, as a joke, knowing it's stupid.)* Maple syrup? You wanna be my little hotcake?

BETH. It's not …

DAVID. What? What is it?

BETH. Nothing. *(Brief pause.)*

DAVID. Oh shit. *(Long pause.)* Beth, there is no God.

BETH. But what if there is?

DAVID. There isn't.

BETH. How do you know?

DAVID. Because.

BETH. Because why?

DAVID. Because if there was a God, Beth, come on, if, if there was a God, then the, uh, the Crusades wouldn't have been allowed to happen; and the, uh Holocaust wouldn't have been allowed to happen. This whole world of shittiness wouldn't have ever been allowed to happen if anyone who really cared was watching.

BETH. *(Overlapping.)* I know what you're saying —

DAVID. *(Overlapping.)* — and we suffer and He just sits there and judges?

BETH. I just can't be as sure as you about everything —

DAVID. I *know* —

BETH. And you weren't raised in the church and I was, and you have to —

DAVID. I *know* that —

BETH. And I know you think that's stupid —

DAVID. I *don't* think it's stupid —

BETH. I just can't be as sure. *(She pulls her shirt closed, crosses her arms and sits there. Long pause.)*

DAVID. OK, so let me get this straight.

BETH. What?

DAVID. *(Trying to make her laugh.)* I'm sorry, I just need to understand what's happening to me right now because my penis is kind of asking me a lot of questions. Three years of being friends, standing next to each other at soccer games; three years of slowly realizing we're married to the wrong people —

BETH. Don't say that.

DAVID. *(With firmer conviction.)* Three years of getting sicker and sicker, vomiting in our hearts from not being with each other, so you're calling me up in tears from your cell phone in the car at midnight, "Brad did this, Brad did that, I need to see you" —

BETH. I know ...

DAVID. And I'm so sad and confused at work I'm filling prescriptions wrong and giving old ladies diarrhea, and everybody's telling me I should go in for an MRI? After three years of that, and making out in cars and making out in bathrooms at parties, and promises, promises, promises, after three years of that I finally get you in a room with me alone, and it's God? This idea?

BETH. I'm sorry. I can't change.

DAVID. Beth, I don't want you to change.

BETH. You do, though.

DAVID. No, I ... look.

BETH. What?

DAVID. I don't want to fight.

BETH. I don't either.

DAVID. I'm here because I'm in love with you, not to fight.

BETH. I know that.

DAVID. And I don't want to make you unhappy.

BETH. I'm not unhappy, I'm just ...

DAVID. What?

BETH. I mean, you don't really want to do this anyway, right? You love Cathy, you love your kids ...

DAVID. Don't tell me what I don't want to do, please —

BETH. Don't be a jerk.

DAVID. Then don't tell me what I don't want to do.

BETH. Well, you *don't, really,* do you? You love Annie and Ruthie and Gus.

DAVID. Annie and Ruthie and Gus are not any happier than I am.

BETH. David, they're the happiest kids I know.

DAVID. Not inside.

BETH. You're weird.

DAVID. No, Beth, they're very uptight. And they know, I swear, they know something isn't right, because they're like always ... consoling me in some odd way, it's creepy.

BETH. And what about Cathy?

DAVID. Cathy ... is a mistake that I made, and I am a mistake that *she* made —

BETH. *(Partially overlapping previous line.)* So am I a mistake

13

you're making? Are you a mistake I'm making?

DAVID. *(Rushing, overlapping.)* I don't love Cathy anymore, Beth, I love *you.* I can't help it.

BETH. And what happens when you don't love *me* anymore?

DAVID. Beth, what do you want me to do? How horrible do I have to feel? Do I wish it was different? Yes. Do I wish I didn't have to make other people miserable in order to follow my heart? Yes. But I can't help how I feel. I love you, I love you more than anything I've ever loved in my life.

BETH. Really?

DAVID. Really. I want —

BETH. Really really?

DAVID. Yes.

BETH. I mean, because, if there was ever a time when you have to be honest with me and yourself, David, it's now —

DAVID. I'm being honest with myself, I want to be with you all the time. My life is so much better when I'm with you, I don't know how to do without you the rest of the time.

BETH. You know what? You're in love with being in love, I think.

DAVID. Oh, does that thought comfort you? Does that make it easier for you to not give in and do this?

BETH. No, it doesn't —

DAVID. Look, I'm sorry I have dreams, I'm sorry I wish life was different —

BETH. You're not the only one —

DAVID. *(Simply, without too much anger.)* Well, you're talking like I'm the only one, "you're in love with being in love" …

BETH. I have dreams too!

DAVID. *(Knowing he's going too far as he says it.)* Well, you don't act that way.*

BETH. David, I'm scared of how big my dreams are and how much they make me feel, and *that's* why, OK, I'm sitting here trying not to do the wrong thing for any of us, OK?

DAVID. It's not your job to keep me out of hell, or keep me safe or something —

BETH. David, I just don't want to lose you as a friend.

DAVID. You won't. You'll never ever ever lose me as a friend.

BETH. *(Referring to * above.)* I don't *believe* you said that.

DAVID. What?

BETH. No.

DAVID. Tell me. Come on. Come on, I'm sorry. Forget it. I'm sorry.

Just say what you want to say. Please. Just say what you want to say.

BETH. Every night I lay in bed next to Brad, you know, and I think about *us*. Every night. Even when I don't want to, when it would be easier to just forget, these thoughts come to me from somewhere underneath everything. I think about you and me and …

DAVID. And what?

BETH. You're gonna think this is stupid.

DAVID. You think about a baby.

BETH. Yes.

DAVID. I think about a baby too sometimes.

BETH. You do?

DAVID. Yes.

BETH. Why didn't you tell me?

DAVID. I didn't want to seem like …

BETH. Like what?

DAVID. Like I wanted you for … having my babies or something. I figured you had enough kids …

BETH. You should have told me.

DAVID. Yeah?

BETH. Yeah, I wouldn't have minded hearing that.

DAVID. Sorry. I think about our baby.

BETH. Me too. *(They kiss a moment, tenderly.)* Last night, I was thinking … you and I and Lily …

DAVID. Lily?

BETH. That's her name, in my head. Lily.

DAVID. Lily.

BETH. Yeah. Lily. She was, like, four years old, with long dark hair and really serious eyes and smart? And we went to the store at Christmastime to get stuff to make cookies —

DAVID. You?

BETH. I know, I can cook, it's a dream! But we all went to the store and it was snowing, those big fat fluffy flakes … dream flakes … and we got stuff to make sugar cookies, and on the way home, she was in her car seat and she reached in the bag and pulled out a little plastic bottle of orange flower water? Which I've read about in Gourmet, you know, but never seen? And she ended up spilling this orange flower water stuff all over the back seat. And you and I had to roll down the windows, the scent was so strong … and the … *(Brief pause.)*

DAVID. What?

BETH. *(Full of longing.)* And the scent of the orangey air and the

15

coolness rushing into the car and you and me happy and Lily in the back … giggling … we were so happy. We were *so* happy. And that's just *one* night of laying there thinking in that bed. I do that *every* night. Every night for the past three years. So don't tell me I don't have dreams, OK?

DAVID. I'm sorry.

BETH. I have dreams. What I don't know is whether us taking this forward is gonna make any of them come true, or if it's just gonna make you hate me and I'll lose you as a friend, and then that'll make everything worse. *(She clasps her bra, buttons her blouse, and swings around to sit on the edge of the bed.)*

DAVID. How could it be worse? You're married to, like, the fucking most —

BETH. David, don't talk about Brad.

DAVID. I'm sorry, that thing you told me the other day, where he was so concerned that you should keep the kids quiet while he watches the *game?*

BETH. He's not easy to live with, I know! And he takes his work very seriously —

DAVID. Oh come on, videos? And I suppose he "needs his time"?

BETH. He does!

DAVID. You've got to be kidding me. "Keep the kids quiet while I watch the fucking game"? That's not good, Beth. That's, like, "Bad Father." That's, like, one step short of *The Shining*. *(By now, Beth has slipped on her shoes and is standing up.)*

BETH. *(Like a bullet.)* David, do you really want to be one of *them?* You think you could really take being one of *them?* *(She points outside, i.e., towards the audience.)* You spent all that time trying to convince me the world out there had disappeared. Why? Because it's full of people who do *this,* David. It's full of people who shit all over each other, and whose word doesn't mean anything, and whose kids are so screwed up, coming home to no Dad or no Mom, and it's all sold to us like it's almost normal, are we really gonna be like them? Isn't that what we're asking each other to do?

DAVID. *(Searching for a way back to her.)* No, we're asking each other for … for a moment of … goodness … in a life that is mostly unpleasant and way too short —

BETH. *(Searching just as hard.)* But there are no moments of goodness that don't … come with responsibilities.

DAVID. I know that.

BETH. I don't think you do. *(After a beat, David lays down on the*

bed and screams into the pillow for a good ten seconds.)
DAVID. *(Into pillow.)* Aahhhhh!
BETH. *(After a beat.)* We should go.
DAVID. *(Looking up from pillow, after a beat.)* You know what my mistake was?
BETH. David, this is not a mistake.
DAVID. You know where I screwed this up?
BETH. David, we're doing the right thing. You have a life. I have a life. Our kids have lives. This is —
DAVID. I never should have talked. Hesitation turns everything into a discussion. And we've been hesitating ever since we met. *(He rises.)* I never should have *talked. (He goes to her, puts his arms around her. They look at each for a while, and then he kisses her. After a moment, she pulls away.)*
BETH. No.
DAVID. *(Giving up.)* OK. OK. *(A moment passes, and then he takes the bottom of her skirt in his hands and pulls it up, and pulls her tightly against him.)* Beth, I can't make it seem right, and I can't make the world go away, and I can't even kid myself it's right. I just *want* you, OK? I want to be *with* you … and *for* you … and *in* you. Right now. OK? *(Brief pause.)*
BETH. *(Almost dizzy.)* OK. *(They kiss. Music rises. David and Beth exit the bed area. Beth sits down in her chair.)*

Scene 3

Brad stands and meets David in a sunny pool of light. They gaze out towards the audience, watching a soccer game.

BRAD. Looks like old Arshavir Blackwell's gonna score our only goal again. Christ, he must absolutely hate fucking life being on this team. *(To the field.)* Go! Now take it downfield!
DAVID. Everybody feeds him the ball, that must be kinda fun for him —
BRAD. I know, but the only reason — *(To the field.)* Don't be scared to get in front of him, Carl! *(To David.)* The only reason his parents have him playing rec soccer at all is to teach him a lesson.

DAVID. Yeah?

BRAD. Yeah, he used to be on a traveling team in the Cities, but they thought he was getting a big head — *(To the field.)* Attaboy, Carl, get in his face! — *(To David.)* so they stuck him with our kids for a season. They live in Albertville so the commute's the same either way. What the hell kinda name is that anyway, Arshavir?

DAVID. I think it's Armenian.

BRAD. If my parents had done that to me, given me a name like that, I woulda taken a shit on the dining room table every night. I woulda crapped 'em out a *great* big bowl of snakes. *(After a beat.)* You played sports? Back in school?

DAVID. Sure. Not soccer, but I, I was on the tennis team —

BRAD. *(Sardonically.)* Yeah, that's a sport. Where's the little woman?

DAVID. Oh, she took, um … Ruthie and Annie started ballet today, so —

BRAD. That new place across from the movie theatre?

DAVID. Yeah —

BRAD. I thought that's what that might be. I wasn't sure, looking in.

DAVID. Yeah, it's a ballet studio.

BRAD. You seen that babe who runs it then?

DAVID. Mmhmm.

BRAD. Would *you?*

DAVID. Oh sure. Totally.

BRAD. I saw her in there painting the other night, a couple months ago, I guess it was, but she was hot. She had on a leotard and all that long black hair. And she's single?

DAVID. I think so, yeah. But I think she might be the girlfriend of that new guy at the radio station, Wigdahl whatever, but —

BRAD. OK, tell me something.

DAVID. OK.

BRAD. *(After much thought.)* Her or … *(He points to a woman nearby.)* Katie Amundson. Desert island, which one do you take?

DAVID. *(A little uneasy.)* I don't know … you tell —

BRAD. Come on, have a fucking conversation with me, which one? *(To the field.)* Hand ball! Ref! Ref! That was a hand ball! *(To David.)* Which one? *(To the field.)* Carl, don't let him get behind you like that!

DAVID. Katie.

BRAD. Yeah, I know, I know, for one night, the other maybe, but — you're right — it's very deceptive — *(To the field.)* Don't be afraid to get hurt, Carl! You can't play afraid! *(To David.)* So. Katie.

DAVID. Yeah. She's got something.

BRAD. I'll tell you what she's got, she's got that ass. She's got that undeniable ass. *(To the field.)* Hey, Gus, nice D! *(To David.)* Did you see that?

DAVID. Yeah. *(To the field.)* Way to go, Gussie!

BRAD. He's a good kid.

DAVID. Thanks.

BRAD. OK. Katie Amundson or … *(He surreptitiously points to another woman nearby.)*

DAVID. Elena?

BRAD. Yeah.

DAVID. Are you serious?

BRAD. You getting picky?

DAVID. No, it's just …

BRAD. See, I *like* that eye.

DAVID. It would drive me crazy, I think —

BRAD. If it went *out,* yeah, like a walleye, yeah, but *in* a little like that's kinda sweet. It's kinda helpless looking, like you could catch her, you know? Like she'd be at the back of the herd, dawdling. *(Brad crosses his eyes.)*

DAVID. No.

BRAD. *(Still with eyes crossed.)* You don't see any charm in this at all?

DAVID. No.

BRAD. See, I'm taking Elena on that one. Does Katie know you feel this way about her?

DAVID. No.

BRAD. You want me to get her over here and you two could set up some time maybe?

DAVID. No. Thanks.

BRAD. Cathy'd bite your balls off, wouldn't she?

DAVID. Oh yeah.

BRAD. So what about Beth? *(To field.)* Go! Go! Go! Go!

DAVID. Your Beth?

BRAD. Yeah. My Beth. Katie or my Beth?

DAVID. *(Bewildered.)* I don't know, what about Cathy?

BRAD. Cathy or Katie?

DAVID. Yeah.

BRAD. For me?

DAVID. Yeah.

BRAD. That's easy, I'll take Cathy. *(Immediately, to the field, clap-*

19

ping.) Good game, you guys! Good game! Way to hustle out there! Good hustle, Arshavir! Good hustle, Carl! *(To David.)* Wouldn't you take Beth?

DAVID. Over Katie?

BRAD. Over Cathy. *(To the field.)* Nice game, Gus! Carl, get your stuff together!

DAVID. Uhh …

BRAD. I'll see you next weekend and hey, by the way, Beth told me to ask you, she knows her insurance won't let her refill her pills until the end of the month, but Oscar got into her purse and ate 'em…?

DAVID. Is he OK?

BRAD. He doesn't seem any sicker than usual. He ate her lipstick and blush and everything.

DAVID. Christ.

BRAD. Yeah, he eats her old tampons if she doesn't cover the bathroom trash tight enough. *(With too much edge.)* It's fucking disgusting. *(Brad puts out his hand to shake.)* Nice talking to you, I'll see you next week. *(They shake hands. As Brad exits, he calls upstage, in a joking sotto voce …)* Hey, Katie, I think David over here wants a word with you! No, I'm just kidding, bye! *(He exits to his chair, followed by a disconcerted David. Music rises. David sits down.)*

Scene 4

Beth stands, goes to the bed area and pulls a suitcase out from under the bed, sets it on the bed, and opens it. She removes several articles of clothing and sets them beside the suitcase on the bed. She changes blouses. Meanwhile, Brad has put on an apron that says "World's Greatest Dad" and he enters the scene carrying a large spatula and a container of charcoal lighter fluid as Beth begins putting the clothes carefully back into the suitcase.

BRAD. Have you seen the other one of these?

BETH. No.

BRAD. I thought I asked you to buy two, we're always running out —

BETH. Gosh —

BRAD. This one's hardly got enough to —

BETH. *(Tense and falsely.)* Gosh, honey, I'm sorry, I must not have gotten around to it.

BRAD. What are you doing? What are you doing?

BETH. What does it look like I'm doing, Brad? I'm leaving.

BRAD. What?

BETH. You heard me, I'm leaving.

BRAD. *(Gesturing to where he entered.)* Because of that down there? Because —

BETH. I'm not stupid, Brad!

BRAD. No, this is funny ...

BETH. The boys aren't stupid and I'm not stupid, and to say something like that —

BRAD. I didn't mean you were stupid, it was just a ... comment, for Christ's sake –

BETH. In front of *my* friends.

BRAD. Beth, they know —

BETH. That you think you can say something like that is so scary to me —

BRAD. Beth, they know I'm a prick, they don't listen to what I say.

BETH. They know you're a prick.

BRAD. Yeah, everybody knows I'm a prick!

BETH. And you're able to live with that?

BRAD. It's who I am! Look, I'm sorry, I — I say things! I don't mean them, I just say them! You know that!

BETH. No, what I know is ... I'm really not happy ... and I haven't been happy for a long time, and that's ... just ... I gotta go. *(She closes the suitcase.)* I gotta go.

BRAD. No.

BETH. What does that mean?

BRAD. It means no, I won't let you go. You can't —

BETH. Do you want me to scream? Do you want to make a big scene with Denny and Sonya downstairs?

BRAD. Go ahead.

BETH. Brad!

BRAD. Denny and Sonya can go fuck themselves for all I care, my wife isn't walking out the door!

BETH. Like I'm some character in a story!

BRAD. What the hell does —

BETH. You say it like I'm some little character in a story, "my wife's not gonna ... " *I'm not some little character in a story! (As she picks up the suitcase and attempts to exit past him, he touches her. She drops the suitcase and screams at the top of her lungs.)* DON'T TOUCH ME! DON'T TOUCH ME! *(He backs off.)*

BRAD. Sorry!

BETH. Every time you touch me, it's like being raped!

BRAD. Jesus Christ, you're a fucking freak!

BETH. No, I'm not.

BRAD. Just tell me where you're going.

BETH. No! It's none of your business!

BRAD. You're gonna run to what's-his-name, your little boyfriend?

BETH. I'm going to the cabin, you don't know what —

BRAD. You're gonna go run to your little fucking boyfriend.

BETH. I don't know what you're talking about.

BRAD. Oh, fuck you!

BETH. No, you think I need someone to run to, like I need somebody, like living in the same house with you for fifteen years isn't enough to make me sick to my stomach? I don't need another reason to be miserable, Brad! You're all the reason anyone would ever need!

BRAD. Beth, I know you and that pharmacist have been fucking around behind my back. I wasn't gonna do anything about it —

BETH. *(Overlapping.)* You are so wrong about —

BRAD. *(Overlapping.)* — because I didn't want the boys to find out their mother was a whore! *(She picks up the suitcase.)*

BETH. You know what, I'm going. You obviously have some idea in your head that is totally of your own creation and — *(He reaches to stop her. Beth, like an animal.)* I SAID DON'T TOUCH ME! *(She starts to go.)*

BRAD. *(A little unnerved.)* So, so, so right in front of Denny and Sonya ...

BETH. Everyone knows you're a prick, Brad! I'm sure they'll take it in stride!

BRAD. He won't leave Cathy, you know that, don't you?

BETH. I'm not even gonna have this discussion because, you know what? I don't know what it's about!

BRAD. He won't!

BETH. *(Suddenly shifting.)* Look, he knows what he wants and I know what I want and we've been very clear with each other —

BRAD. Aha! So you *are* fucking this guy!

BETH. Yeah, Brad, I guess I am, I'm "fucking this guy!"

BRAD. Oh, maybe I shouldn't use such bad language, you're right. It's such a beautiful thing when two people who are married to other people can put their stinky little parts in each other, I'm sorry if I made it sound cheap! Fuckin' A!

BETH. I know it's cheap.

BRAD. Oh, you do?

BETH. Yes, I *know* it's not good —

BRAD. But you *don't* know there's no way he's leaving those three little kids? Come on! You've gotta know *that*, right? He's never gonna leave those kids. That bitch wife of his has him wound around her finger tighter than a Duncan fucking yo-yo. Have you ever seen him with her at the store picking out movies? It's Merchant Ivory, Jane Austen, Merchant Ivory, Jane Austen, English every single fucking time, he's not going *anywhere!* You *must* know that, Beth. You're not stupid, you *must*. *(After a beat.)* So look, let's go downstairs and have a beer and —

BETH. No!

BRAD. Come on, you can bitch to Sonya, Denny and I'll take the boys to the lake for a swim or something —

BETH. NO!

BRAD. Do you want me to just send 'em home?

BETH. No. I don't know!

BRAD. Look, let me go down there and tell 'em we need a little time —

BETH. No!

BRAD. Yes, I'll let them get the coals started, maybe Denny can figure out how to use that thing of yours where it works without fluid and we'll ... I'll be right back up. *(Brief pause.)*

BETH. *(Resignedly.)* Whatever. *(Brad exits and sits in his chair. Beth carries the suitcase back into the room and sets it down. She sits on the edge of the bed and bursts into tears. She cries for a minute or two; then stands and looks around the room at all the things she'll be leaving. Note: This whole sequence should take longer than is normal — for a play — or comfortable. Then, finally, Brad rises and enters the scene again, having taken off his apron.)*

BRAD. They decided to go home.

BETH. I'm sorry. I'll call Sonya later and explain —

BRAD. No, they understand, it's not a big deal.

BETH. It's a big deal, Brad.

BRAD. You know what I mean.

BETH. What did you tell them?

BRAD. I said you're fucking the pharmacist at Sundberg's and we gotta talk.

BETH. You did not.

BRAD. No, I didn't, I just said we had to talk, that's all. And they took the boys.

BETH. Where?

BRAD. I don't know, they'll go to Perkins or somewhere and have some dinner I guess. *(Brief pause.)*

BETH. God.

BRAD. What?

BETH. Everything actually has to happen, doesn't it? You think in your mind things can happen without happening, but in the end, they always have to actually happen. Actual kids have to get driven away by actual friends ... and actual people have to sit there and actually ... live. *(Brief pause.)*

BRAD. So you know for a fact he's leaving Cathy?

BETH. *(Beaten down.)* God, I don't know, Brad. And I don't care, we're ... this is not about that. That's as much of a mistake probably as this was, I'm the queen of romantic mistakes —

BRAD. You and me.

BETH. What?

BRAD. A mistake?

BETH. Yeah!

BRAD. It wasn't a mistake for me.

BETH. What am I supposed to say to that?

BRAD. Nothing, but that's ...

BETH. All of a sudden you have feelings...?

BRAD. *(Honest.)* No, it's just what I'm saying. Is it perfect all the time? No way. But it's not a mistake. But you, you really think —

BETH. Look ... do you really want to have this conversation? Because, truthfully, I just want to go.

BRAD. Then go! Fuck it! *(He screams fiercely, right in her face.)* Go! Go! Go! Go!

BETH. *(Overlapping.)* Don't you understand, you stupid idiot, this doesn't make me happy?

BRAD. *(Overlapping.)* Go! Go! GO! GO! GO!

BETH. Don't you understand that? If I felt like I had a choice, I'd ... I'd have one! *(A pause. He steps away from her. After a moment, Beth rises.)*

BRAD. *(Still angry.)* You're going up to the cabin?

24

BETH. Yeah.

BRAD. Is he gonna be up there?

BETH. No.

BRAD. *Yes.*

BETH. I don't know! Does it matter?

BRAD. Yes, it's my fucking cabin! I built it! I don't want some shit-for-brains pharmacist fucking my wife in that cabin!

BETH. Then he won't come up!

BRAD. I'm just asking for the common courtesy of not having him spray *his* come all over *my* pillow!

BETH. I said he won't come up, shut up about it already! I wasn't planning on it anyway, but —

BRAD. Thank you!

BETH. God! You're such a pig!

BRAD. Does Cathy know?

BETH. *I don't know!* I told you, that's not what this is about! This is you and me, Brad! David or no David —

BRAD. Fuck, don't you say that name in my house ...

BETH. David or no David —

BRAD. *Don't say that motherfucker's name in this house, Beth!*

BETH. He doesn't know what I'm doing, I haven't told him about this. It's not like we're on walkie-talkies all the time, it's not that serious.

BRAD. So you don't know if Cathy knows?

BETH. No, I don't, and I don't care.

BRAD. Because the minute you walk out the door, I'm gonna call over there and tell her her husband is fucking my wife.

BETH. Is that supposed to make me stay? You want me to stay with you for his sake?

BRAD. I don't know, Beth! You're the one who said this shit has to actually happen! All I'm saying is, walk out the door and things will start to actually fucking happen!

BETH. And you have to hurt everybody else?

BRAD. Yeah, I do!

BETH. This is not about them!

BRAD. Bullshit! Bull-fat-fucking-bull-*shit!* We were happy —

BETH. We were never happy, Brad, like people are supposed to be —

BRAD. Bullshit! We were happy for fifteen years —

BETH. I was never happy!

BRAD. Is that what he tells you, that you've never been happy?

BETH. No!

BRAD. This *wonderful* guy —

BETH. It's the *truth!*

BRAD. He takes half your fucking life and pisses all over it just so he can get in your pants, getting you to believe you've never been happy? We've fucked in this bed, shit, how many times, Beth? A thousand times? Two thousand times? And you're fuckin' telling me you've never been happy? What, that you fuckin' faked it *every* time? Just tell me you faked it every time! Every time you said you loved me, every time you pushed that pussy of yours in my face and said you loved me —

BETH. There's more to life than sex, you *idiot!*

BRAD. *(A sudden rush, a new thought.)* And you *owe* me nothing?

BETH. What?

BRAD. I made a promise to you and I've kept it all these years and you owe me *nothing?*

BETH. I've cleaned your house and fed you and fed your kids and made sure everything —

BRAD. I'm talking about a *promise* —

BETH. If anything, you owe *me* —

BRAD. I'm not talking about housework, I'm talking about a *promise!* I took my life, I could have done whatever I wanted to with it, but I chased you down — stupid fucking me — and you never let me forget that — "oh, he had to chase me down" — "I wasn't really ready, but he was *so persistent*" — and stupid me, I chased you down because I thought you were the most beautiful woman I'd ever seen in my life and I thought, "Shit, Brad, you *are* an idiot, but maybe, just maybe, she'll see something in you that you don't even see, you know?"

BETH. I know, I'm the worst thing that ever happened to you, I know that!

BRAD. *Nobody,* none of my friends thought you'd go out with me, I remember Slick said it was a "logical impossibility" —

BETH. And it still is, that's the problem!

BRAD. So why did you say "yes"? You bitch! Why did we have kids? Why did you waste my time for the past fifteen motherfucking years?

BETH. Because I didn't know what else to do! And I didn't think I would ever be good at anything! And I didn't think it would last this long!

BRAD. Oh, should I have died? Did I miss my cue?

BETH. No, it's just ... *life gets long sometimes!*

BRAD. You know, you're full of shit!

BETH. I am not full of shit, Brad, I'm just tired of being married to you, and that's all it is! It's nothing as complicated as you seem to want to make it.

BRAD. You loved me!

BETH. I didn't love you, I was scared to live!

BRAD. No, you loved me, you did! And when this whole thing turns to shit on you, you're gonna know that too, in the pit of your fucking heart, you're gonna know it like you never knew anything! *(He picks up the phone.)* What's his number?

BETH. Don't call him.

BRAD. What's his fucking number?

BETH. Brad, if you wanna be mad at somebody, be mad at me! *(She tries to hang up the phone.)*

BRAD. Don't touch that fucking phone again!

BETH. Look, you want me to stay, I'll stay, but — *(Again, she tries to hang up the phone.)*

BRAD. I said, don't touch this fucking phone! *(He pushes her away.)* You think it feels like being raped every time I touch you? I'll throw you down and fuck you right now, you fucking cunt!

BETH. I'm leaving. Before you do something that gets you locked up in prison. Because that wouldn't be good for the boys. *(She picks up the suitcase.)*

BRAD. *(Yelling.)* Oh, do us all a favor!

BETH. I am!

BRAD. *(Yelling.)* Save me from *myself!* What a fucking joke!

BETH. You can stop yelling, Brad, I'm leaving!

BRAD. *(Top of his lungs.)* Go ahead! And I'll tell the boys when they get back all about their mother the fucking whore! *(Beth goes upstage and sits down in her chair. Brad yells in her direction. Even louder, so all the neighbors can hear.)* I oughta screw you right through this bed and straight down to Hell where you came from, you fucking cunt! You motherfucking cunt! (Music rises. He dials the phone, waits. Still rattled, his voice hoarse.)* Hi, Audrey. Pull up David Calhoun on the computer. What's his number? Thanks. *(He waits. He hangs up. He dials. He waits.)* Hi, is this Cathy? Yeah, this is Brad Youngquist. Yeah, from the video store. No, I know, there's, it's not overdue yet, listen, I just thought you should know your husband's fucking my wife. *(He slams down the phone, sits on the bed. Lights shift as music rises.)*

Scene 5

After a brief pause, Brad rises slowly from the bed and moves into a pool of light downstage.

BRAD. Dear Beth. The boys are staying at Denny and Sonya's tonight, the house is a mess, and I'm a little drunk. ("No, you're a big drunk," I can hear you say in my mind.) As you of all people know, I'm not very good with words. And I know I'm not easy to live with. But I hope you'll give me another chance. I'm willing to put all of this shit behind us if you'll give me another chance. I want another chance. I need another chance. You're the best thing that has ever happened to me in my life, and I can't believe I'm sitting here on the edge of losing you forever. If you're really happier with the pharmacist, then I guess you should be with him, but I really hope that after a few days up there at Chez Youngquist, you'll want to come home to me. I'll build you your own bathroom up there, if you want. I love you, Beth. I'm not perfect, but I do love you the best I know how, and I can learn and change and be better, if you'll just come home. You are so pretty. Looking around right now, I see you are the pretty part of everything here. Without you here, this place is really a dump. And I don't mean cleaning-wise. You know what I mean. Please come home if you want to and we will be lovers again. From the bottom of an ocean of that awful beer your brother makes and which I finally got desperate enough to take a crack at ... your biggest fan ... Brad. *(Brad exits and sits down in his seat. Music continues.)*

Scene 6

David and Cathy are on the bed. The atmosphere is one of grim, slightly absurd resignation. Note: This entire scene should be done quietly enough to indicate that neither participant wishes to wake the children.

CATHY. I'm not going to tell the kids for you.

DAVID. I wouldn't ask you to.

CATHY. Oh, I think you would. I think you were just about to.

DAVID. I wasn't.

CATHY. It's going to seriously mess up Gus.

DAVID. I'll work it out with him.

CATHY. The girls I can handle, I can train them not to hate men — I would have had to do that anyway — but Gus, I don't have access to him.

DAVID. I don't either, really —

CATHY. *That's* an excuse.

DAVID. Look, I said I'll talk to him! I'll talk to them in the morning.

CATHY. Then I'll leave the house, because I don't think I can take it.

DAVID. Look, do you want me to go?

CATHY. No. *(Long pause.)* You know what I want?

DAVID. What?

CATHY. You want to do what I want? You want to console me? Make yourself feel better?

DAVID. What? *(She crawls on top of him, clearly trying to initiate sex. Brief pause.)* I can't.

CATHY. Why? Because you don't "love" me anymore? Your license to say shit like that has been permanently revoked.

DAVID. Cathy, this won't stop me from leaving.

CATHY. Oh, stop being so vain. Did it ever occur to you that maybe I'm glad to be rid of you? You're such a shit to the kids lately anyway, David, it's probably all for the best.

DAVID. Honey, I think you're a little confused. *(She slaps his face hard.)*

CATHY. No. I'm not. I know exactly what I'm doing. OK?

DAVID. OK. *(Straddling him, she begins slowly moving her hips up and down. Just a little.)*

CATHY. Give me your hands.

DAVID. No.

CATHY. Come on, hold me up a little. *(After a moment, He offers his hands. They link hands.)*

DAVID. I can't get it up. I won't. I can't.

CATHY. You're so noble. It's touching. Let's get Beth on the phone and tell her how you're enduring this trial so gallantly by refusing to get an erection.

DAVID. This really doesn't seem like you.

CATHY. David, you're so self-involved, I don't think you really know what seems like me or doesn't seem like me anymore.

DAVID. You might be right.

CATHY. Hold me around the back.

DAVID. No! Just … get off me …

CATHY. David, if you want to go stay somewhere else, then do it, but if you're gonna stay here, then …

DAVID. What?

CATHY. *(After a long beat.)* Get on the team!

DAVID. "Get on the team."

CATHY. Yes! Get on the team … you jerk. *(Brief pause. He laughs a little, she laughs back, and he relents, puts his hands on her behind, beneath her nightgown. She continues moving above him. After a while, she leans down and kisses him. He does not respond. She begins kissing his face, shoulders, and chest every now and then.)* How is it with Beth?

DAVID. What?

CATHY. The sex.

DAVID. You don't want to know.

CATHY. Yes I do.

DAVID. It's great.

CATHY. It's easy for it to be great when you don't have to watch the person pee every morning.

DAVID. So I should wake up and realize Beth won't do it for me once I've got her all to myself, twenty-four hours a day.

CATHY. That, and the self-hatred for what you've done to the kids. And Brad showing up every morning to take a shit on your porch.

DAVID. Did he tell you that?

CATHY. Yeah.

DAVID. That guy is fascinated with shitting on things. I think he must hold his tension in his ass, that's why he's always got prostate problems.

CATHY. And where do you hold yours?

DAVID. My tension?

CATHY. Mmhmm.

DAVID. The obvious answer is my dick, I guess, I don't know, you obviously have a plan —

CATHY. I think you hold it in me.

DAVID. I hold *my* tension in *you*. That's a trick.

CATHY. Isn't it? See, I think, in little ways you ask me to hold it for you, and I do, and then you hate me for helping you, so you run off and generate passionate feelings for other women.

DAVID. There are no other women, it's just Beth. It's always been just Beth.

CATHY. Katie Amundson.

DAVID. Did you and Brad have dinner or something together?

CATHY. We had coffee.

DAVID. Where?

CATHY. At Sundberg's.

DAVID. You shit!

CATHY. It wasn't my idea. It was Brad's, he said he wanted to infiltrate the enemy camp.

DAVID. Right in front of everybody at Sundberg's?

CATHY. David, it's a free world! You've proved that. It's a great, big, ugly, free world. *(Long silence. Suddenly they kiss with real abandon, tinged with anger, for the first time. After a while, she pulls back.)* Today in class, I was handing back tests ...

DAVID. Yeah?

CATHY. I'd given them this very simple ear training test, just for fun, and little Jason Pearson, he said, "Mrs. Calhoun? I got nine out of twenty-five. Is that good?" So I sent him down to Ed's room, I said, "Go ask your math teacher."

DAVID. You still like teaching?

CATHY. I do. It's ... you know what it is, ultimately? I think it's as simple as I enjoy the company of kids. *(After a moment.)* You know who doesn't like school, though ...

DAVID. Ruthie.

CATHY. She was complaining to me today about how all her teachers expect her to be perfect. She said, "The more I do better, the more they expect me to do better. It's too much." She said that about twenty times, staring into the rear view mirror like this total drama queen: "It's too much. It's too much."

DAVID. Are you trying to make me sentimental about the kids? It's working.

CATHY. I'm just telling you about your children, David. I'm not as cagey as you think.

DAVID. You're the smartest person *I* know.

CATHY. I am not.

DAVID. No, you know what I mean. You're smart about bullshit.

CATHY. So why do you want to be with her? You want somebody dumb?

DAVID. She's not dumb. She's just a little more naïve than you.

31

CATHY. She'd have to be, to think you could actually love her.

DAVID. I do love her.

CATHY. Uh huh.

DAVID. I do.

CATHY. David, can you please reach a little inside me and do your part? *(He's nonplussed.)* What?

DAVID. I don't know, you've never been this direct before.

CATHY. Well, our marriage is essentially over, right?

DAVID. I think so, yeah.

CATHY. You're leaving me for Beth, right, you two are gonna go be boyfriend and girlfriend?

DAVID. I hope so.

CATHY. Then do I really need to waste my dignity on you?

DAVID. OK. *(He does something beneath her nightgown which registers a non-verbal response.)*

CATHY. Thank you. *(A few moments without words pass.)* I thought you said you couldn't get it up.

DAVID. Honey, this is just making me sad.

CATHY. Look, unless you want me to start screaming … at the top of my lungs … and have the children come running in here … and watch you pack your bags right now, you'll shut up, OK? *(Brief pause.)*

DAVID. OK. *(Brief pause.)*

CATHY. I want you inside me. *(David sighs.)* Shit, David, would you please stop pretending to care? Picture *her.* Or Katie Amundson.

DAVID. I don't have to picture anybody else.

CATHY. Don't do me any favors.

DAVID. I do think you're pretty.

CATHY. *(Quoting* The Rainmaker.*)* "You're pretty, Lizzie. You're pretty."

DAVID. Shut up!

CATHY. You shut up! *(A moment passes. Through a silent agreement, over the course of ten seconds or so, they work together to get him inside her.)*

CATHY. There. Isn't that better?

DAVID. Better than what?

CATHY. Fighting.

DAVID. It feels like fighting to me. I feel like I'm getting the shit beat out of me. *(Brief pause. As the scene continues, the pace of their physicality accelerates slightly, their words more and more broken up by breaths and silences. This acceleration is gentle, however, and the volume is never loud enough to wake up the kids.)*

CATHY. It was actually fun … having coffee with Brad. He's such a palooka, he's kinda sweet.

DAVID. He's not very sweet to Beth.

CATHY. Poor her. But he's not as dumb as you think, David. He's known about you two for a long time, long before he called.

DAVID. She told him?

CATHY. No, don't worry, your little sweetie didn't betray your confidence. He just knew. He told me … he told me the day he figured it out, he was driving by Warehouse Foods … and he saw a man and a woman loading groceries into the back of a car. One was lifting them out of the cart and then handing them … handing them to the other one to put into the trunk. And he said it suddenly occurred to him, "I bet they think they're two different people."

DAVID. What the hell does that mean?

CATHY. That's what I said. He said for one second, it looked to him like they were really one person, but with two bodies. But one person. Connected. By invisible threads. And that's when he knew.

DAVID. Brad said this.

CATHY. Yeah.

DAVID. The video store guy.

CATHY. Yeah, I know. But what it made *me* think was … what I didn't tell *him* … what it made me think was … maybe we're *all* the same person. Maybe all of us … *(Their lovemaking escalates.)*

DAVID. Are you OK?

CATHY. I'm OK. Are you OK?

DAVID. I'm OK. *(After two minutes of wordless intercourse, they both have orgasms. She collapses onto him. A long time passes in silence.)* I'll tell the kids in the morning. *(Brief pause.)*

CATHY. *(With great sadness but no tears.)* Fine. *(After a moment or two, she begins to cry. He moves to put his arms around her. She sits up a little, still on top of him, and pushes his arms away. Still crying.)* No! I don't want any sympathy. I don't want any of your shitty little sympathy. *(Brief pause. He wipes her tears away as they fall on his face.)* Sorry. *(She settles back down onto him. He does not embrace her; his arms lay stretched out impotently at his sides. A moment. Then music rises. Lights shift.)*

Scene 7

David and Cathy rise from the bed and get dressed. Once dressed, David goes upstage to his seat. Beth rises, wearing a raincoat and carrying an umbrella, and meets Cathy downstage in a pool of grey light. Sounds of rain and periodic thunder can be heard; nothing too threatening. They are both focused on the soccer field. Cathy is eating candy from a small bag.

CATHY. That Arshavir is something else, isn't he?
BETH. *(Uncomfortable.)* Uh, I just thank God, for Carl's sake, he's on the team.
CATHY. Gussie, too.
BETH. He's a natural.
CATHY. *(To the field.)* Get in there, Gus! Good man! *(Brief pause. Thunderclap and the sound of intensified rain.)* Mind if get under there? Just for a second?
BETH. Uhh, sure. *(Cathy gets under the umbrella next to Beth.)*
CATHY. *(After a beat.)* You want some Sour Skittles?
BETH. No, thanks.
CATHY. Gus tells me they're the biggest thing to happen to candy since Gushers. They're not bad.
BETH. *(After a beat.)* I'll try one. I've seen the commercials, I was wondering. *(Cathy gives her some candy. They eat a moment in silence. After a beat, Beth holds out her hand for some more.)* Just, like, two.
CATHY. See what I mean?
BETH. Yeah. *(Brief pause as they chew.)*
CATHY. So look, what am I doing over here with candy, I'll tell you, I'm the one who's gonna be taking over your "Meals On Wheels" route.
BETH. At First Lutheran?
CATHY. Yeah, I figure now that David's out of the house, I don't care, I'm gonna at least join a church and get 'em baptized. *(Gently facetious.)* So they don't rot in Hell.
BETH. Yeah, I think that's good.
CATHY. You can tell him, too, if you want —

34

BETH. I don't … whatever. You can tell him.

CATHY. Anyway, I just wanted to warn you, I'll be the one showing up at the church to get trained-in, so don't freak out.

BETH. I could get someone else to do it, if you want — I mean — it's pretty much nothing —

CATHY. No, I think that's what church is for, right?

BETH. For … ?

CATHY. For breaking down the barriers we put up in the world? Between people?

BETH. Are you serious?

CATHY. Yeah. I mean, it should be; that's the point, right?

BETH. In theory.

CATHY. Well … here's a barrier.

BETH. Yes, here is one, you're right.

CATHY. *(To the field.)* You have to run, Gus! You have to actually run! *(Cathy offers Beth more candy.)* More? *(Beth takes a few.)*

BETH. Thanks.

CATHY. *(To Beth.)* But you, you're quitting.

BETH. Yeah, who told you that?

CATHY. *(Overlapping.)* Pastor Ed.

BETH. *(After a beat.)* Why did he tell you that?

CATHY. Why are you quitting?

BETH. *(After a beat.)* Are you really asking me?

CATHY. Yeah.

BETH. This is a real conversation?

CATHY. Yeah.

BETH. And you're asking me because …

CATHY. Because I want you to know you don't have to quit because of me and the kids, that's all. I wouldn't want that.

BETH. Wouldn't you?

CATHY. No.

BETH. I'm quitting because …

CATHY. David's making you.

BETH. No. I'm quitting because when I try to pray now … I feel stupid.

CATHY. *(After a beat.)* I think everybody feels that way. It's a stupid thing to do.

BETH. Do you pray?

CATHY. Sometimes. Not as much as I used to. But sometimes.

BETH. *(Very absently, with an eye on the soccer game.)* When I was really little, you know … I thought God was like my Dad, only

35

bigger. And, uh, just like it felt to walk through our house where my Dad had built all the furniture, that's how it felt to walk through the whole world. Everything seemed like it had a little note taped to it: "Thought you might like this tree!" "Thought you might like this sunset!" "Thought you might like this cute boy! I made him just for you!" *(Beth looks to Cathy, who smiles a little.)* And, uh, I told my guidance counselor in high school, you won't believe this, I told her I didn't need to choose a career, because God had a plan for my life? And she said she was part of how God let people *in* on His plans. And I believed her. And *that* was the beginning of the end ... because after that, it was so easy to see everything that way, right? Making out in the back of Jeff Kosternople's VW Bus seemed like God's way of letting me *in* on something; and drinking too much in college was God's way of letting me *in* on something. And now, just when I would really love to look out over those trees, Cathy, and see a little note: "Hi Beth! Thought you might like this world" — I look around and there are no notes on anything, anywhere. *(After a beat.)* Cathy, I'm really sorry about what's happened. If it ever felt like a choice, I'd have chosen differently, but it never did. I'm sorry.

CATHY. *(Abruptly.)* Are you going to keep the kids?

BETH. *(A little chastened.)* Not if Brad has his way ... his lawyer's really good, it's kinda scary —

CATHY. So it'll just be you and David?

BETH. Yeah —

CATHY. Because you should know, he's had a low sperm count the past few years. *(Beth doesn't know what to say.)* We were trying up until two years ago to have one more. He blamed me until we went to a doctor in the Cities and did the tests, but who knows, if he's happier with you, maybe that'll bring it back up. It works that way sometimes —

BETH. Cathy, listen —

CATHY. *(Plunging on, her bitterness showing through.)* — in which case, if it does, let me tell you, he's very good with babies, loves babies, but once they're no longer helpless, Beth, he blames them for everything, he can be very petty when it comes to —

BETH. *(Harder.)* Cathy. *(Cathy stops.)* I really don't want to have this conversation.

CATHY. Oh. OK. *(She takes a few steps away.)* But I'll see you on Wednesday.

BETH. Yeah. I guess. I'll show you how to feed the old people.

CATHY. Beth, I hate to tell you this, but I think we *are* the old people. *(Cathy exits upstage to her chair. Music rises. Lights shift as Beth enters the bedroom area and joins David there. Lights shift.)*

Scene 8

David and Beth are standing in the bed area, both wearing light jackets.

BETH. It's a nice house.
DAVID. I like the trees. I killed every tree at our house within about three years of moving in. It'd be fun to have trees again.
BETH. Something to kill.
DAVID. No, I'd be better to these trees. *(Brief pause as they look around the room.)*
BETH. It would be nice to have a few more bedrooms.
DAVID. *(A little edgy.)* I know, but it's all about what we can afford at this point —
BETH. I just —
DAVID. What? *(Referring to the realtor.)* Just say it, she's downstairs staring into that pager of hers. Say it. I know what you're gonna say.
BETH. *(Whispering.)* I can't have Carl and Kevin thinking they don't have their own room at Mommy's house.
DAVID. And what about my kids?
BETH. I feel the same for them.
DAVID. Oh, you do?
BETH. Yes.
DAVID. The exact same.
BETH. David, don't start that again —
DAVID. Look, we both know, this is how much house we can afford right now, did we have the conversation or not? Did we sit there and add it all up or not?
BETH. David, if Carl and Kevin don't feel at home here now, if we don't make it a welcoming place for them now, they'll never feel like they belong.
DAVID. So what do you want me to do?

BETH. I don't know!

DAVID. If you know this is how much house we can afford, then what are you asking me to do?

BETH. I'm not ... asking you to do anything!

DAVID. It seems like you are!

BETH. No, I just said I wish there were more bedrooms!

DAVID. Which is an indictment of me.

BETH. No, it's a fact.

DAVID. No, it's not, it's an indictment of me.

BETH. Would you stop? We're choosing to do this and it's ... it's just hard to face the limits of it, that's all.

DAVID. And the limits are set by the fact I don't make enough money to buy a house with six bedrooms, or however many you think would be enough for everyone to feel "at home!" It's an indictment of me!

BETH. If you want to see it that way, for some sick, self-destructive reason —

DAVID. There's no other way to see it!

BETH. That's not true!

DAVID. Yes it is! You don't want to work, so my salary is it, my salary is the border of what's possible —

BETH. I have told you I'm willing to work if it's —

DAVID. No! I don't want you coming home every day, tired and miserable, and blaming it on me! He didn't make you work, I'm not gonna make you work. I won't have you hating me for that. Shit. *(He sits on the bed.)* Isn't this fun. *(Brief pause.)* My kids would like their own rooms too, you know.

BETH. I know. *(Brief pause.)*

DAVID. Shit shit shit.

BETH. I'm sorry I brought it up.

DAVID. To have to ... to have to be in this situation at this point in my life ... to be starting everything over is just really discouraging sometimes, you know?

BETH. I think it's sort of fun.

DAVID. Then why do you bring up impossible things I can't do anything about? If it's so fun?

BETH. I wasn't —

DAVID. You don't think it's fun, anyway, that's a shitty patronizing thing to say.

BETH. If I can't be honest with you about what I care about, David, then who can I talk to about it? Who?

DAVID. You can talk to me, but could you do it without accusing me of keeping your kids from feeling at home?

BETH. I never said — *(Brief pause.)* Forget it. *(Longer pause.)* Look. Do you like this house?

DAVID. I like it OK. I wish we could get something bigger too, something closer to the lake, like your place —

BETH. But given all that, do you like this house?

DAVID. Yeah, I like it. I like the trees.

BETH. Then let's buy it.

DAVID. No, it doesn't have enough bedrooms.

BETH. David —

DAVID. No, look, you're right, it doesn't have enough bedrooms —

BETH. David, stop. Listen. We'll have a summit meeting with the kids. And we'll let them decide together how to decorate that other bedroom, we'll get two bunkbeds, we'll let them divide up the drawers, we'll put them in charge of everything. What we can't give them in terms of space, we'll give them in terms of autonomy.

DAVID. Don't try to make it better.

BETH. I'm not.

DAVID. Yes you are, you're being like a prairie wife.

BETH. And you're being kind of a jerk.

DAVID. Look, I'm sorry, but I didn't fall in love with you so you could be brave and resourceful. I wanted to give you things and treat you better than your asshole husband, not ... force you to make excuses for why we can't treat your kids like members of the family.

BETH. Your kids, too.

DAVID. I know, but I can carry that, I've been disappointing my kids ever since they were born. Disappointing you is a new feeling. And I don't like it.

BETH. You want to go back to our kingdom in the clouds.

DAVID. I wouldn't mind.

BETH. With the apples like tall ships, sailing ...

DAVID. It was better. It was simpler.

BETH. No it wasn't. We were lying all the time and sneaking around.

DAVID. I didn't mind the lying.

BETH. I did.

DAVID. You would've gotten used to it.

BETH. No, I was nervous all the time, and rushing around trying to fit you into my schedule ... I never got the grocery shopping really totally done the whole time we were seeing each other ... it was hell.

DAVID. But now you get it done.

BETH. Yes!

DAVID. That's great. Christ, I can feel it starting all over again.

BETH. What does that mean?

DAVID. Just what you said, Beth, it's exactly what you said. We've done it, we've become like them. We're the ones who break up families and buy shitty furniture to fill up ugly houses, we're the ones who ruin the world all for the chance to have sex with someone we want to have sex with. *(Brief pause.)* Don't look that way.

BETH. Is that what you think this is?

DAVID. Isn't it? I mean, I have feelings, but underneath the feelings, what else is it?

BETH. It's love, I thought —

DAVID. "Love."

BETH. I thought that's what it was anyway.

DAVID. *(Overlapping.)* Love that tears everything in its path apart. Love that deprives innocent children of their parents.

BETH. Oh my God …

DAVID. Don't get that tone in your voice please. It's so fucking dramatic.

BETH. I knew this would happen …

DAVID. Beth, would you please spare me your fragility just this once, just this once?

BETH. I have left my children —

DAVID. I've left mine too!

BETH. Don't tell me I can't have feelings about that, about how much I've set aside!

DAVID. See, this is how it starts, we're not even in the goddamn house and it's "how much you've set aside" …

BETH. David, if you're not comfortable with thinking you're worth it —

DAVID. Don't make it about me!

BETH. Then what —

DAVID. It's what we have together, if it's anything, but I can't take it being about me!

BETH. Then what we have together —

DAVID. Which it might not even *be* —

BETH. If you can't live with what it costs me to be with you, then we shouldn't do this!

DAVID. *(Loud.)* Maybe you're right, maybe we shouldn't! *(Long silence. Quieter.)* Maybe it's all a big mistake. *(Brief pause.)* When I sat Gus down and told him I was moving out ... you know what I felt? I felt ... this is terrible to even say ... I felt ... I enjoyed making him sad.

BETH. No you didn't —

DAVID. Yes I did, that's who I am now, I was being all sympathetic but inside I was saying, "See, you little shit, this is how hard it's been for me ever since the day you were born and cemented me into this marriage; now you live with it for awhile and see how it feels." I felt that feeling behind the words; behind all the sadness and sympathy, there was just ... smallness.

BETH. I don't believe that.

DAVID. You don't feel any resentment at all ... towards them?

BETH. Of course I do, David, they're my kids! But it's been ... I know you don't want to hear things like this, because I'm not supposed to feel anything that makes you feel guilty, but ... living without those guys is breaking my heart, resentment and all, it's breaking my heart! I thought I knew what heartbroken was —

DAVID. But being with me has taught you.

BETH. That's not what I'm saying —

DAVID. But that's what the situation *is!*

BETH. You know, *you're* the one a person can't say anything around, you're the one who's fragile —

DAVID. I'm the one who's realistic!

BETH. *Then it's too late to be realistic!*

DAVID. No it's not! You can go back to Brad.

BETH. I don't want to go back to Brad!

DAVID. You want to go back to your boys!

BETH. Yes I do! But I can't!

DAVID. Why? Just go back! Suck it up! Deal with it! I certainly don't want to spend the rest of my life with someone who's this unhappy!

BETH. Neither do I!

DAVID. Then go back! Why don't you just go back?

BETH. *(Whispering fiercely, full of hate and desperation.)* Because I'm pregnant, you fucking jerk, you selfish selfish selfish fucking jerk! Because I'm pregnant. (Brief pause. He reaches out to her.) Don't. Don't touch me. Don't you ever ... ever ... ever touch me again. *(She wipes her eyes as she cries.)* God. I'm so alone. *(Brief pause. David goes to her. He moves to put his arms around her.)* No.

DAVID. Come on. I'm sorry. Come on. Please. Please. I'm sorry.

(She moves closer to him. He very gently puts his arms around her.)
BETH. It's all so hard.
DAVID. Yeah. It is. *(They hold each other for a long moment. Then they both look up suddenly towards where the door to the room would be.)*
BETH. Shit. *(They step apart. Wiping her eyes, pulling herself together.)* Here she comes.

Scene 9

Beth exits the bedroom area. David picks up the stuffed tiger from the beside table and then steps into a pool of light downstage.

DAVID. Dear Lily. *(Music rises.)* Life goes by so quickly I thought I would take a moment today to sit down and write you a letter. You can't read yet, but I am going to put this in the box Mommy keeps all your pictures in, and you can read it when you're older. Long before you were born, Mommy used to have dreams about you. And she would tell them to me, and we would have so much fun sitting quietly, talking about what you'd be like. It was almost as if you were our friend before you were ever really here. Of course, we didn't really know you then. We didn't know your first word would be "purple," or that you would like eating lamb so much, or that you would be such a great singer. It has been a real treat to find out all the ways we were wrong about you and right about you, and you continue to surprise us every day. Lately, when we put you to bed, you make us say, "Tweety tweety, co-co-coconut, ga ga goo goo, bo bo bo bo, I love you, see you in the morning, sleep well, good night, sleep tight, don't let the bedbugs bite, that's right, that's all, sweet dreams, work well, think twice." And we don't know where you came up with this.

Today is a very special day, because it is Christmas Eve. You are so excited! You have asked Santa for a Barbie doll, a puppy, and a tiger — we'll see what happens. But the best news is, today one of Mommy's dreams about you came true. We went to the store this afternoon, and the traffic was very busy and it was snowing, and we got flour and butter and sugar to make cookies. And we got something very strange called Orange Flower Water, to make the cookies smell pretty. In Mommy's dream, you spilled the orange flower water in the back seat — we didn't know then that you would be a good girl who wouldn't do that — but we rolled down the windows anyway as we drove back to our apartment and poured out some of it on the seats, and we were all so happy our hearts almost flew out of us and took off. *(Light shift and Cathy, Brad, and Beth rise and step downstage, aware of David, but facing the audience, their varying degrees of implacability standing in contrast to whatever small note of unadulterated positivity David strikes.)*

What also was different today from Mommy's dream is it was a little sad. Because Mommy and Daddy hurt a lot of people's feelings, and made your half-brothers and half-sisters very sad, just for the chance to be together. And they all visited us this morning, and you cried when they left, because you love them so much and they are very sweet to you. And this is one of life's great mysteries, Lily, my dear little pumpkin seed, and I cannot explain it, but somehow people are always hurting each other and love keeps happening. It just keeps happening. And the longer you live and the more you notice this, the harder it gets to know what's right and wrong. Sometimes it almost seems impossible. All I know is we would not change anything that ever happened, ever, because I am so excited to know you and Mommy and we can't wait to see what you are going to do with your amazing life. *(Brad, Cathy, and Beth leave the stage as David continues.)*

So. That's all. I am wrapping this letter around this little bottle of orange flower water — (Mommy's cookies didn't really turn out so good) — so you can smell it again when you are bigger and you want to remember all the mixed-up reasons that go into making a miracle like you. Whatever happens to you ever in this life, always remember we love you, Lily, and you are worth *everything*. *(A moment passes. David puts the stuffed tiger on the bed and exits. Lights slowly fade. A pool of light lingers on the tiger as the music rises. Blackout.)*

End of Play

PROPERTY LIST

Suitcase (BETH)
Several articles of clothing (BETH)
Extra Blouse (BETH)
Large spatula (BRAD)
Container of charcoal (BRAD)
Lighter fluid (BRAD)
Pillow (DAVID)
Telephone (BRAD, BETH)
Umbrella (BETH)
Bag of candy (CATHY)
Small orange Beanie Baby tiger (DAVID)

NEW PLAYS

★ **MOTHERHOOD OUT LOUD by Leslie Ayvazian, Brooke Berman, David Cale, Jessica Goldberg, Beth Henley, Lameece Issaq, Claire LaZebnik, Lisa Loomer, Michele Lowe, Marco Pennette, Theresa Rebeck, Luanne Rice, Annie Weisman and Cheryl L. West, conceived by Susan R. Rose and Joan Stein.** When entrusting the subject of motherhood to such a dazzling collection of celebrated American writers, what results is a joyous, moving, hilarious, and altogether thrilling theatrical event. "Never fails to strike both the funny bone and the heart." –*BackStage.* "Packed with wisdom, laughter, and plenty of wry surprises." –*TheaterMania.* [1M, 3W] ISBN: 978-0-8222-2589-8

★ **COCK by Mike Bartlett.** When John takes a break from his boyfriend, he accidentally meets the girl of his dreams. Filled with guilt and indecision, he decides there is only one way to straighten this out. "[A] brilliant and blackly hilarious feat of provocation." –*Independent.* "A smart, prickly and rewarding view of sexual and emotional confusion." –*Evening Standard.* [3M, 1W] ISBN: 978-0-8222-2766-3

★ **F. Scott Fitzgerald's THE GREAT GATSBY adapted for the stage by Simon Levy.** Jay Gatsby, a self-made millionaire, passionately pursues the elusive Daisy Buchanan. Nick Carraway, a young newcomer to Long Island, is drawn into their world of obsession, greed and danger. "Levy's combination of narration, dialogue and action delivers most of what is best in the novel." –*Seattle Post-Intelligencer.* "A beautifully crafted interpretation of the 1925 novel which defined the Jazz Age." –*London Free Press.* [5M, 4W] ISBN: 978-0-8222-2727-4

★ **LONELY, I'M NOT by Paul Weitz.** At an age when most people are discovering what they want to do with their lives, Porter has been married and divorced, earned seven figures as a corporate "ninja," and had a nervous breakdown. It's been four years since he's had a job or a date, and he's decided to give life another shot. "Critic's pick!" –*NY Times.* "An enjoyable ride." –*NY Daily News.* [3M, 3W] ISBN: 978-0-8222-2734-2

★ **ASUNCION by Jesse Eisenberg.** Edgar and Vinny are not racist. In fact, Edgar maintains a blog condemning American imperialism, and Vinny is three-quarters into a Ph.D. in Black Studies. When Asuncion becomes their new roommate, the boys have a perfect opportunity to demonstrate how open-minded they truly are. "Mr. Eisenberg writes lively dialogue that strikes plenty of comic sparks." –*NY Times.* "An almost ridiculously enjoyable portrait of slacker trauma among would-be intellectuals." –*Newsday.* [2M, 2W] ISBN: 978-0-8222-2630-7

DRAMATISTS PLAY SERVICE, INC.
440 Park Avenue South, New York, NY 10016 212-683-8960 Fax 212-213-1539
postmaster@dramatists.com www.dramatists.com

NEW PLAYS

★ **THE PICTURE OF DORIAN GRAY by Roberto Aguirre-Sacasa, based on the novel by Oscar Wilde.** Preternaturally handsome Dorian Gray has his portrait painted by his college classmate Basil Hallwood. When their mutual friend Henry Wotton offers to include it in a show, Dorian makes a fateful wish—that his portrait should grow old instead of him—and strikes an unspeakable bargain with the devil. [5M, 2W] ISBN: 978-0-8222-2590-4

★ **THE LYONS by Nicky Silver.** As Ben Lyons lies dying, it becomes clear that he and his wife have been at war for many years, and his impending demise has brought no relief. When they're joined by their children all efforts at a sentimental goodbye to the dying patriarch are soon abandoned. "Hilariously frank, clear-sighted, compassionate and forgiving." –*NY Times.* "Mordant, dark and rich." –*Associated Press.* [3M, 3W] ISBN: 978-0-8222-2659-8

★ **STANDING ON CEREMONY by Mo Gaffney, Jordan Harrison, Moisés Kaufman, Neil LaBute, Wendy MacLeod, José Rivera, Paul Rudnick, and Doug Wright, conceived by Brian Shnipper.** Witty, warm and occasionally wacky, these plays are vows to the blessings of equality, the universal challenges of relationships and the often hilarious power of love. "CEREMONY puts a human face on a hot-button issue and delivers laughter and tears rather than propaganda." –*BackStage.* [3M, 3W] ISBN: 978-0-8222-2654-3

★ **ONE ARM by Moisés Kaufman, based on the short story and screenplay by Tennessee Williams.** Ollie joins the Navy and becomes the lightweight boxing champion of the Pacific Fleet. Soon after, he loses his arm in a car accident, and he turns to hustling to survive. "[A] fast, fierce, brutally beautiful stage adaptation." –*NY Magazine.* "A fascinatingly lurid, provocative and fatalistic piece of theater." –*Variety.* [7M, 1W] ISBN: 978-0-8222-2564-5

★ **AN ILIAD by Lisa Peterson and Denis O'Hare.** A modern-day retelling of Homer's classic. Poetry and humor, the ancient tale of the Trojan War and the modern world collide in this captivating theatrical experience. "Shocking, glorious, primal and deeply satisfying." –*Time Out NY.* "Explosive, altogether breathtaking." –*Chicago Sun-Times.* [1M] ISBN: 978-0-8222-2687-1

★ **THE COLUMNIST by David Auburn.** At the height of the Cold War, Joe Alsop is the nation's most influential journalist, beloved, feared and courted by the Washington world. But as the '60s dawn and America undergoes dizzying change, the intense political dramas Joe is embroiled in become deeply personal as well. "Intensely satisfying." –*Bloomberg News.* [5M, 2W] ISBN: 978-0-8222-2699-4

DRAMATISTS PLAY SERVICE, INC.
440 Park Avenue South, New York, NY 10016 212-683-8960 Fax 212-213-1539
postmaster@dramatists.com www.dramatists.com

NEW PLAYS

★ **BENGAL TIGER AT THE BAGHDAD ZOO by Rajiv Joseph.** The lives of two American Marines and an Iraqi translator are forever changed by an encounter with a quick-witted tiger who haunts the streets of war-torn Baghdad. "[A] boldly imagined, harrowing and surprisingly funny drama." *–NY Times.* "Tragic yet darkly comic and highly imaginative." *–CurtainUp.* [5M, 2W] ISBN: 978-0-8222-2565-2

★ **THE PITMEN PAINTERS by Lee Hall, inspired by a book by William Feaver.** Based on the triumphant true story, a group of British miners discover a new way to express themselves and unexpectedly become art-world sensations. "Excitingly ambiguous, in-the-moment theater." *–NY Times.* "Heartfelt, moving and deeply politicized." *–Chicago Tribune.* [5M, 2W] ISBN: 978-0-8222-2507-2

★ **RELATIVELY SPEAKING by Ethan Coen, Elaine May and Woody Allen.** In TALKING CURE, Ethan Coen uncovers the sort of insanity that can only come from family. Elaine May explores the hilarity of passing in GEORGE IS DEAD. In HONEYMOON MOTEL, Woody Allen invites you to the sort of wedding day you won't forget. "Firecracker funny." *–NY Times.* "A rollicking good time." *–New Yorker.* [8M, 7W] ISBN: 978-0-8222-2394-8

★ **SONS OF THE PROPHET by Stephen Karam.** If to live is to suffer, then Joseph Douaihy is more alive than most. With unexplained chronic pain and the fate of his reeling family on his shoulders, Joseph's health, sanity, and insurance premium are on the line. "Explosively funny." *–NY Times.* "At once deep, deft and beautifully made." *–New Yorker.* [5M, 3W] ISBN: 978-0-8222-2597-3

★ **THE MOUNTAINTOP by Katori Hall.** A gripping reimagination of events the night before the assassination of the civil rights leader Dr. Martin Luther King, Jr. "An ominous electricity crackles through the opening moments." *–NY Times.* "[A] thrilling, wild, provocative flight of magical realism." *–Associated Press.* "Crackles with theatricality and a humanity more moving than sainthood." *–NY Newsday.* [1M, 1W] ISBN: 978-0-8222-2603-1

★ **ALL NEW PEOPLE by Zach Braff.** Charlie is 35, heartbroken, and just wants some time away from the rest of the world. Long Beach Island seems to be the perfect escape until his solitude is interrupted by a motley parade of misfits who show up and change his plans. "Consistently and sometimes sensationally funny." *–NY Times.* "A morbidly funny play about the trendy new existential condition of being young, adorable, and miserable." *–Variety.* [2M, 2W] ISBN: 978-0-8222-2562-1

DRAMATISTS PLAY SERVICE, INC.
440 Park Avenue South, New York, NY 10016 212-683-8960 Fax 212-213-1539
postmaster@dramatists.com www.dramatists.com

NEW PLAYS

★ **CLYBOURNE PARK by Bruce Norris.** WINNER OF THE 2011 PULITZER PRIZE AND 2012 TONY AWARD. Act One takes place in 1959 as community leaders try to stop the sale of a home to a black family. Act Two is set in the same house in the present day as the now predominantly African-American neighborhood battles to hold its ground. "Vital, sharp-witted and ferociously smart." –*NY Times.* "A theatrical treasure…Indisputably, uproariously funny." –*Entertainment Weekly.* [4M, 3W] ISBN: 978-0-8222-2697-0

★ **WATER BY THE SPOONFUL by Quiara Alegría Hudes.** WINNER OF THE 2012 PULITZER PRIZE. A Puerto Rican veteran is surrounded by the North Philadelphia demons he tried to escape in the service. "This is a very funny, warm, and yes uplifting play." –*Hartford Courant.* "The play is a combination poem, prayer and app on how to cope in an age of uncertainty, speed and chaos." –*Variety.* [4M, 3W] ISBN: 978-0-8222-2716-8

★ **RED by John Logan.** WINNER OF THE 2010 TONY AWARD. Mark Rothko has just landed the biggest commission in the history of modern art. But when his young assistant, Ken, gains the confidence to challenge him, Rothko faces the agonizing possibility that his crowning achievement could also become his undoing. "Intense and exciting." –*NY Times.* "Smart, eloquent entertainment." –*New Yorker.* [2M] ISBN: 978-0-8222-2483-9

★ **VENUS IN FUR by David Ives.** Thomas, a beleaguered playwright/director, is desperate to find an actress to play Vanda, the female lead in his adaptation of the classic sadomasochistic tale *Venus in Fur.* "Ninety minutes of good, kinky fun." –*NY Times.* "A fast-paced journey into one man's entrapment by a clever, vengeful female." –*Associated Press.* [1M, 1W] ISBN: 978-0-8222-2603-1

★ **OTHER DESERT CITIES by Jon Robin Baitz.** Brooke returns home to Palm Springs after a six-year absence and announces that she is about to publish a memoir dredging up a pivotal and tragic event in the family's history—a wound they don't want reopened. "Leaves you feeling both moved and gratifyingly sated." –*NY Times.* "A genuine pleasure." –*NY Post.* [2M, 3W] ISBN: 978-0-8222-2605-5

★ **TRIBES by Nina Raine.** Billy was born deaf into a hearing family and adapts brilliantly to his family's unconventional ways, but it's not until he meets Sylvia, a young woman on the brink of deafness, that he finally understands what it means to be understood. "A smart, lively play." –*NY Times.* "[A] bright and boldly provocative drama." –*Associated Press.* [3M, 2W] ISBN: 978-0-8222-2751-9

DRAMATISTS PLAY SERVICE, INC.
440 Park Avenue South, New York, NY 10016 212-683-8960 Fax 212-213-1539
postmaster@dramatists.com www.dramatists.com